Brenda S. Jackson, PhD

Foreword by Dr. James H. Vick, II

Detroit, Michigan USA

Reflections in Prison Ministry
Copyright © 2017 Brenda S. Jackson, PhD

All Scripture quotations, unless otherwise indicated, are taken from the Holy Bible, New International Version®, NIV®. Copyright ©1973, 1978, 1984, 2011 by Biblica, Inc.™ Used by permission of Zondervan. All rights reserved worldwide. www.zondervan.com The "NIV" and "New International Version" are trademarks registered in the United States Patent and Trademark Office by Biblica, Inc.™

All rights reserved. No part of this publication may be reproduced, stored in a retrieval system, or transmitted in any form or by any means – electronic, mechanical, photocopy, recording, or any other – except for brief quotations in printed reviews, without the prior permission of the publisher.

*Priority*ONE Publications
P. O. Box 361332 | Grosse Pointe, MI 48236
E-mail: info@priorityonebooks.com
URL: http://www.priorityonebooks.com

ISBN 13: 978-1-933972-52-7
ISBN 10: 1-933972-52-1

Editing by Patricia Hicks
Cover and Interior design by Christina Dixon

Printed in the United States of America

Table of Contents

Foreword by Dr. James H. Vick, II..5
Introduction..7

PART I ~ Reflections of The Callings
Team Reflections:
    Dr. Brenda Simuel Jackson 17
    Brenda Rudolph..21
    Deacon James Douglas...25
    Elder Arnoldine Lancaster 27
    Trustee James Galloway 31
    Debra Pollard 35

PART II ~ Why Prison Ministry is Needed
Learning Reflections:
    Prison Ministry Needed...41
    What is Prison/Jail?..42
    Who Are Those to Whom We Minister? 45

PART III ~ What is Prison Ministry?
The Question is, What is Prison Ministry? 53
My 2002 Journal of Jail Ministry 55
BSJ Christian Seminars, Inc. 501c3...63

PART IV ~ Reflections on Prison Ministry Abroad
South Africa – January 2011 69
Lusaka, Zambia – December 2011...75
Ndola, Zambia – May 2013..83
Ndola, Zambia – June 2014 91
Durban – July 2015 105
Swaziland – May 2016 111

Appendix..123
Bibliography...127
About the Author...129

FOREWORD

As the Academic Dean of Jacksonville Theological Seminary, it is an honor to recommend "Reflections in Prison Ministry" by one our Alumni, Dr. Brenda S. Jackson. This book would be an excellent source of wisdom for anyone desiring to answer the calling in prison ministry.

Dr. Jackson graduated from Jacksonville Theological Seminary's Divinity program which is designed to equip men and women of God for this type of Ministry. The extensive knowledge and work put into this book would prove to be a valuable tool for those who desire to have an impact on those who are imprisoned.

Dr. James H. Vick, II
Academic Dean

INTRODUCTION

The foundational scriptures supporting prison ministry are found in the Old Testament and the New Testament. These scriptures point to salvation.

Isaiah 42:7b, c
"...to free captives from prison and to release from the dungeon those who sit in darkness."

Isaiah 61:1b-2
"...proclaim freedom for the captives and release from darkness for the prisoners."

Philemon 11,16
"Formerly he was useless...now he has become useful... no longer as a slave, but better than a slave, as a dear brother.

John 8:36
"So if the Son sets you free, you will be free indeed."

Prison ministry points those incarcerated to a road to freedom:

- Freedom from the penalty of sin.
- Freedom from negative personhood.
- Freedom from hopelessness.
- Freedom from lack of self-confidence to succeed.
- Freedom from fear of failure.

PART I

Reflections on The Callings

Freedom for the Prisoners
©2016 Brenda Simuel Jackson

We cannot open the prison gates
to usher you out of your plight.

We cannot judge you as wrong or right.

We can share with you a plan that will direct you
from the dark side of life's oppressions
to a light that removes all of your depressions.

Our goal is to help you
remove the stain of sin and condemnation,
and to bring joy and eternity without condemnation.

Our goal is true freedom that is of the Spirit.

Our goals are true righteousness
that comes with forgiveness.

Prison ministry is our tool
to being witnesses that God can use.

Team Reflections

Man is born in sin and shaped in iniquity (Psalm 51:5). This is a familiar scriptural reference for Christians; however, I did not expect this to be a fundamental peg (one of four) of the early penal philosophy. In order to justify punishment for crime, Christian influence was a force. The four assumptions that dominated penal philosophy were:

1. The causes of crime are located within the individual.

2. People should be punished for their inappropriate actions.

3. Behavior is modifiable.

4. Isolated institutions are the appropriate setting in which to modify those behaviors." (Beckner & Park, 5)

A goal of mine at one stage in my life was to be an institutional Chaplain with the Michigan Department of Corrections. My journey was most definitely prison ministry but as a volunteer chaplain. The Lord knows the end from the beginning. Currently, not only am I a volunteer in prison ministry, but I volunteer through an organization, Bible Speaks Jesus Christian Seminars, Inc. which contracts with the Bureau of Federal Prisons, and I assist the Chaplain in a residential re-entry program. Chaplains function like missionaries raising their own financial support, or operating out of what the Lord has made possible.

Reflections in Prison Ministry

I received training in restorative justice from Prison Fellowship International, South Africa. Restorative Justice is justice that heals[1] (Beckner & Park, 18). Redemption for the prisoner includes the outside community which facilitates healing. This stresses the need for prison ministry.

The emotion of shame is one of the keys to the success of restorative justice for the offender. In this context, it is shame, not sorrow that can lead to repentance.

Characteristics of criminal thinking were all new revelations learned on this journey in prison ministry. Criminal thinking is closed. This thinking is non-receptive to different ways or alternative methods, does not accept criticism, and does not disclose. Viewing self as a good person in spite of one's deviant behavior is criminal thinking (Ibid, 33) Criminal thinking is likely to say, "I can't," but mean "I won't" do anything disagreeable to me. Trying is out of the question. (Ibid, 35). The criminal mind will not acknowledge fears, but they do exist. This has helped to guide me in the ministry.

The Church within the prison is part of the body of Christ, and outside churches should partner with the church inside the prison to help in outreach. As volunteers, we are always reminded to leave inside what one did not bring in, and take out what one brought in. The impact of this rule on the partnership of churches (inside and out) does not include God's truths. I can

---

[1] Park, Jeffrey, and W. Thomas Beckner. *Effective Jail & Prison Ministry for the 21st Century.* Charlotte, NC: Coalition of Prison Evangelists Publication, 1998. Print. p. 18, 33, 35

testify that ministry with the inside church is having a positive impact, and we do leave it there.

I started in prison ministry in 1991 and was ordained as a Chaplain in 2010. I did not get involved in ministering to juveniles in the Youth Detention Center until approximately 2011. Characteristics of juveniles have similar characteristics but in different degrees as the adults. These include:

> a. The lack of an identity resulting from growing up without a father figure to which one can identify.
>
> b. They have no concept of Christianity and are biblically illiterate.
>
> c. They have no concept of being successful.
>
> d. They are described as having irrational fears.

I believe prison ministry does make a positive impact on the sin nature of all who are not free.

"Recognizing The Call"
By Brenda Simuel Jackson

525 Clinton Street, the place of the Old County Jail,
Division II

The place where I recognized God's call,

and was told, it was true.

The basement where service was held

that Sunday Afternoon,

Was only bright because of the souls

that filled the room.

The out of tune piano, no one could play,
but we sang with gusto anyway.

My sermon, Jesus is The Light, was short and sweet,
one soul said yes, and I did weep.

A road called to travel, I continue on to this day,
Jesus is The Light Who can be seen night or day.

Reflections on the Call
Brenda Simuel Jackson

It was in the late seventies that I was first introduced to a ministry for those incarcerated. My brother-in-law was convicted of second degree murder and sentenced to ten years. During the time of his incarceration, my husband died (1975), and Joe was permitted to attend the funeral.

I felt the need to provide him comfort. This was a time when inmates called collect. Joe called, and I attempted to give encouragement. Soon others from the prison were calling and making threats because of debt owed by Joe. I got scared, and refused all calls, even those from Joe.

Years passed. I became a Sunday school teacher and involved in ministering to the deaf. One member of the deaf community was incarcerated, but was released to Northville State Hospital. I visited her there and ministered to her and other members present. There was always a nagging in my conscious to minister to those incarcerated. I convinced myself that incarcerated did not necessarily mean prison.

In 1989, I was appointed to the deaconess ministry. The spark for prison ministry remained. My Pastor and our church were part of the Metropolitan Jail Ministry, and in the same year, I was invited to minister at Wayne County Jail. It was a year later that I accepted the invitation, and there was no fear. My first official visit

Team Reflections

was in November of 1990 and has been continuous since that date. Ministries ranged from letter writing, correcting Bible Study assignments through CrossRoads Bible study, to providing prison worship services, seminars and Bible Studies in jails, prisons and detention centers.

It was in 1995 that I announced to my Pastor, Rev. R. A. Allen (deceased), my call to the ministry. He anointed me as a missionary to the imprisoned, and he put me in charge of the prison ministry. The seeds of my passion for prison ministry started with the need of an inmate needing encouragement and needing the Word of God. I am often reminded of the Scripture in Matthew 25:44 "Then the righteous will answer Him, Lord, when did we see you hungry, and feed you, or thirsty, and give you something to drink? When did we see you a stranger and invite you in, we needing clothes and clothed you? When did we see you sick or in prison and go to visit you? The King will reply, 'I tell you the truth, whatever you did for the one in the least of these brothers of mine, you did for me!'" Jesus said in Luke 4:18b, "He has sent me to proclaim freedom for the prisoners...." All need to hear that they can be freed from the bondage of sin.

All need to hear that Jesus loves them.

There is still joy in knowing seeds are sown, souls are encouraged, and a need to visit Jesus in prison is fulfilled.

Reflections in Prison Ministry

At times I question myself, as I wonder, is the passion still alive? I read the written comments given to me regarding my visits, (see appendix A). When I see the success of those who are ex-offenders, the joy leaps forward.

Testimony of My Life in Prison Ministry
Brenda Rudolph

How did I become involved in Prison Ministry?
In Ephesians 4:1, Paul challenges us to live lives worthy of the calling we have received from God. As a servant of Christ, I always had a desire to serve the Lord. I would reply to various human right's causes. Unfortunately, I discovered it was **"MY CAUSE"** and not directed by the **HOLY SPIRIT.**

However, in the summer of 1984 while driving from work, I was listening to a radio program titled "Chaplain Ray" who interviewed various inmates whose lives were transformed as a result of Jesus Christ. This became my daily radio station program while driving home. Each day I listened to the various testimonies of how the Gospel set men who were physically bound inside prison walls, spiritually free. While on my drive from work one day, I had a conversation with the Lord. I said to Him, **"Lord, I would love to minister to prisoners."** Since that conversation with the Lord, years had passed. I spent most of my time in prayer and studying God's Word. Six years later, I joined the Jail Ministry at my church. The first time in 1990, when I walked into the Wayne County Jail in Hamtramck and the loud sound of the jail doors slammed behind me, the Holy Spirit brought back the conversation I had with the Lord in 1984, when I said, **"Lord, I would love to minister**

to prisoners." That was the beginning of my twenty-six-year journey in prison ministry.

How has Prison Ministry Benefited Me?

Twenty-six years of prison ministry has provided me with countless benefits that will always be embedded in my memory bank. The best benefit is knowing that I no longer look for my calling, but I'm walking in the calling that Paul described in Ephesians 4:1.

Another benefit of prison ministry is putting God's Word into action by obeying Matthew 25:34-46. When I visit various prisons, I see human lives transformed by the Word of God. Each time we visit local, state, federal and international prisons, the inmates always say, "Thank you for coming and please come back!" This statement raises my motivational level of ministry to the point where my physical body is saying **"NO"** but the spiritual man is saying **"Yes."** For instance, one night I did not want to visit the Wayne County Jail because one of my co-workers had just been killed by her spouse as a result of domestic violence. Sitting in my kitchen at home I told the Lord that I was not going to the jail. But the Holy Spirit kept tugging at my heart and said, "Why are you serving Me?" Before the night was over, I left running to the jail. Once I was at the jail, one of the inmates said, "I have been waiting for you to let you know God answered my prayer through you. Thank you."

Finally, the most important benefit in prison ministry is presenting the Gospel to the unchurched prison population and visibly seeing God transforming lives that were on the path of destruction into new creations in Christ Jesus (2 Cor. 5:17).

Why do I continue in Prison Ministry?

Over these twenty-six years, the challenge of Prison Ministry has been overwhelming to the point that I wanted to QUIT! Once I learned it was **NOT ABOUT ME BUT THE LORD**, I suddenly realized that the Holy Spirit was the One keeping me and not myself. Another reason why I continue in the ministry is when the Holy Spirit allows me to witness to inmates being released from prison, I tangibly see the fruit of my labor. When I have been out and about in the community, the Lord allows me to experience inmates who have been released into the community. For instance, a few times while out in the community, pumping gas, in a party store, in a church service, or waiting in the doctor's office, I have run into former inmates. They would provide me with updates of their lives since being released. It was always a good report. Therefore, God's unexpected events provide the incentive to keep His servant pressing toward the mark of the high calling in Christ Jesus.

Reflections on My Participation in Prison Ministry
Deacon James Douglas

I have been a volunteer in the prison ministry with BSJ Christian Seminars, Inc for about four years. The locations I have ministered in are Huron Valley Women's State Facility, Wayne County Jail, Division 2, Milan Federal Prison and Muskegon State Prison.

Following my retirement from Ford Motor Co. in 2007, I found more time to volunteer and perform community service. I thought about volunteering at a local hospital, but I concluded that I would be duplicating my duties as deacon of New Prospect Missionary Baptist Church.

As the years rolled by, the call to serve in prisons got stronger. I had a brother who was incarcerated in Alabama previous to my retirement, and I ministered to him. I was aware of a prison ministry team to which some of my church members belonged. I discussed, mostly with team member, James Galloway, some of His experiences and just what was required, for about a year. I also spoke to Dr. Brenda S. Jackson, the team director.

Finally, in 2012, the call to serve was strong and clear. I joined the BSJ Christian Seminar Team, initially serving Huron Valley location.

Now, four years later, whenever I sit and reflect on my motivation to continue in the prison ministry, I come back to the following revelations:

Reflections in Prison Ministry

1. The Bible verses, Luke 4:18; 2 Corinthians 5:9-10

2. The opportunity to proclaim God's Word in a defined forum

3. My participation represents positive action and contributes to possible change in the lives of brothers and sisters in need

4. I'm following in the footsteps of my mother who was avid in support of my brother during His incarceration. Also, my Aunt Annie who served tirelessly for many years in prison ministry in Alabama.

In conclusion, let me express that I didn't get involved in prison ministry just to fill up my time. Rather I believe I have been called by God to do this work.

Prison Ministry Reflections
Elder Arnoldine Lancaster

MY CALL to prison ministry began one Sunday morning at Bethesda Missionary Temple Church during morning service. An announcement, from one of the associate ministers, asking for volunteers for the prison ministry, stirred something within me. This was not the first time I had heard the plea for volunteers, but something was different for me. I knew immediately that this call was for me.

After the service, I attempted to get more information. My name was taken and a telephone call promised, but nothing ever came of it. I tried to volunteer several more times but to no avail. I thought that maybe prison ministry was not for me. I stopped trying. A year or so later, I attended a meeting for Angel Tree, and the guest speaker, Joe Williams, was there to speak on His program, Transition of Prisoners. He was asking churches and individuals to get involved in the many aspects of prison ministry. Finally, he gave me the information I needed, and I contacted the person who set up the dates for new volunteers to be trained. God's plan is never thwarted. I was put on a waiting list; several years later I was called to attend a training session. At last, I was getting involved.

I met Minister Norene Snow at the training meeting; she was a member of Bethesda Missionary Temple also. She was already involved in prison ministry and had a team that did weekend seminars at Jackson State Prison and Milan Federal Prison on a monthly basis. The team also did weekly services at Jackson. She invited me to join her team. Sometime later, we were invited to Ryan State Prison to do weekly services.

Why am I still involved?
Why do I travel miles around Michigan and even go as far as Africa to bring the Good News to those incarcerated? Because it is what my God has called me to do. Not only that, I have never come out from one of the services the same way I went in. The anointing of the Spirit of the Lord is always in each service I have attended. Not only are the inmates attentive and appreciative but they also love the Word of God, and they encourage us to continue doing what we do for the Lord.

Dr. Brenda S. Jackson, my mentor, has opened so many doors for our team. She is the one who keeps the Ministry alive and growing. She is the one who mapped out trips to Africa's prisons to share the Gospel with inmates there. She continues to encourage the team to be prepared, be on time, and end on time. She is also why I am still involved.

I don't take Prison Ministry for granted. Prayer and study of the Word are very important. The men and women who we minister to are expecting a Word from God and to learn, not to be entertained. I can't see a time when I am not doing something with Prison Ministry; it is such an important part of my life.

What are my rewards?
Seeing the growth in inmates that we see bi-weekly or monthly, as they grow, so do I. Seeing a former inmate by chance and him or her sharing what a blessing the team made in their lives. Being told to never stop doing what we do, because even though some seem

uninterested, they come, they hear the Word, and some have made drastic changes in their lives. I may never know the difference that the team has made in the lives of those incarcerated, but God knows that's what matters. I love what I do and will continue until God tells me different.

Reflection - Jail and Prison Volunteer
James Galloway

Some volunteers have a great burden ministering to inmates in the rough environment where they are incarcerated. Volunteers put in a great deal of time sharing the Word of God, listening to prisoners' concerns and problems, while doing their best to steer the inmate(s) in the right direction – which is away from certain elements during their incarceration and release into the community.

I decided to become a jail and prison volunteer after visiting two Michigan Correctional Facilities. The first facility was the Ionia Correction Facility in 2003 with Deacon Otis Sheard, who was teaching Bible study. The second visit was in Jackson Correctional Facility, Jackson, MI. This was a "Bill Glass BEHIND THE WALLS" Christian ministry based in Dallas which trains volunteers to share the Gospel of JESUS-the-CHRIST, and then they take volunteers into prisons and jails to share their faith to inmates. In 2009, I joined the BSJ Christian Seminars. The questions I had after the visits and during my first year with BSJ were: Can James Galloway make a difference? This required me to put myself aside and let JESUS be revealed or glorified so HE could have an impact or improve one inmate's life. The second question, what is the possibility of James Galloway solving "a" problem? I was not considering several problems only "one." A very good centering statement attributed to Ralph Waldo Emerson: *"The purpose of life is not to be happy. It is to be useful, to be honorable, to be compassionate, to have made some difference that you have lived and lived well."*[2]

This statement reminds me of the apostle Paul. Paul was jailed but continued to preach and proclaim the Word of God. Some individuals have stated to me that Scriptures referencing jail and prison ministry are for those Christians who are incarcerated for preaching and proclaiming God's Word and not for non-Christians who have committed crimes.

My response was Matthew 28:18-20, "The Great Commission." In Matthew 28:18-20, Jesus was given authority over heaven and earth. Therefore, as a follower of Jesus, I am to go everywhere, to the far corners of the earth, to spread the Gospel.

> "In His previous ministry, Jesus deliberately restricted His work to the Jewish people (Matthew 15:24) and previously sent His disciples with the same restriction (Matthew 10:6). Only on rare exceptions did Jesus minister among the Gentiles (Matthew 15:21-28). Now all of that is in the past, and the disciples are commissioned to take the gospel to all the nations. There is no place on earth where the gospel of Jesus should not be preached and where disciples should not be made."[3]

---

[2] 1988, The Inventurers: Excursions in Life and Career Renewal by Janet Hagberg and Richard Leider, Third Edition, Section 3: Lifestyles, Subsection 10: Spirit, Quote Page 105, Addison-Wesley, Reading, Massachusetts. (Verified on paper)

[3] Guzik, David. "Study Guide for Matthew 28 by David Guzik." *Blue Letter Bible*. Web. 14 June 2017
https://www.blueletterbible.org/Comm/guzik_david/StudyGuide_Mat/Mat_28.cfm

Team Reflections

My second response is that the Apostle's Creed states that Jesus descended into hell. Some theologians will use Matthew 12:38-41; Romans 10:7, Ephesians 4:7-10, and 1 Peter 3:18-20 to demonstrate Christ's descent in hell. If Christ went to hell to preach to the spirits, I can proclaim HIS Word to the incarcerated believers and non-believers that it may have an impact on their criminal behavior.

Every Christian may not be an evangelist in the strict sense of the word, but God has blessed all humans with a certain gift that can fulfill the requirements of Matthew 28:18-20. I believe no life is beyond Jesus' reach. Many inmates and ex-inmates, along with their family are being redeemed by Jesus' love. It is my job to aid the inmate in becoming a spiritual leader within their family, community and job/work environment when they return to their community.

Jail and prison volunteers are seen as a resource to some correctional facilities and as an aid to the inmates in coping with the trauma that inmates face. The trauma may be feeling guilt, anger, shame, hopeless, and/or dealing with a conflict. For some inmates, the volunteer(s) may be the only visitor they will have during their incarceration.

The government should update some of their in prison programs such as education, training, and post release guidance in order to meet the needs of inmates returning to their community. Also, inmates that have served their sentences and returning home should not be denied their voting rights. There is no legal reason for keeping a person who has served their time from voting. It has been shown in Georgia and California that the pre-college and college course taken in prison reduces the recidivism rate. Inmates enrolled in these courses improve their skills so that when they are released they have a better opportunity for employment.

Thus, I have been a volunteer for the jail and prisons for seven years. Some years have not been good to me, but the majority have been excellent. I have been able to help some inmates grow in Jesus, while others remain the same. Many pastors and ministers tell me that they cannot stand to hear the sound of the metal doors closing behind them and this is the reason why they do not do prison ministry. Therefore, those of us who can go behind the prison walls are blessed by God. The question that usually comes from pastors and ministers is, "Are you doing any good?" My response is, "Only God knows; I am a deliverer of His Word."

"It's the action, not the fruit of the action that's important. You have to do the right thing. It may not be in your power, may not be in your time, that there'll be any fruit. But that doesn't mean you stop doing the right things. You may never know what results come from your action. But if you do nothing, there will be no result." **(Mahatma Gandhi)**[4]

---

[4] "Mahatma Gandhi · Move Me Quotes." *Move Me Quotes.* N.p., n.d. Web. 14 June 2017. http://www.movemequotes.com/tag/mahatma-gandhi/

Why Service the Incarcerated?
Deborah Pollard

No one could have told me that I would be a part of the Prison Ministry at my church. If anyone would have suggested that I would be member of a group of individuals that routinely visit various penal institutions to teach and to share the Word of God, I would have thought they had lost their minds. Yet...I am indeed a part of such a group, a very dedicated and wonderful group of Christians, and I enjoy what it is that we do immensely.

I don't know about my Prison Ministry colleagues, but I sincerely feel that God was preparing me for this work during my formative and career years. I worked in Public Health that required hands-on work in our communities, neighborhoods, and many poor homes. I often encountered individuals who were doing whatever they could to survive; often partaking in activities that were illegal. In the inner city, it was nothing to hear people say that the hustle, legal or otherwise, was necessary for survival. These activities, so they thought, were the only road to survival available to poor people, both black and white. Years of exposure I had with the various community personalities is one reason I feel comfortable working with the prison population.

I also spent most of my career training and teaching adults how and why an honest work ethic was the true road to life success. I watched my entire family achieve security and contentment through the slow and steady work route. I feel that that same slow and steady moral ethic will bring the imprisoned closer to a sense of peace, purpose, and closer to God. This can be achieved anywhere. We, who are not incarcerated, are often imprisoned in our minds due to our mental, emotional, and spiritual prison cells. To me, the environments are very similar and allows me to be able to relate to the prison inmates.

I am also the type of individual that works well independently. I find this work very well suited for an individual like me who does not thrive well working in groups.

Most importantly, when I must prepare a lesson for the inmates, it allows me to grow from the prepared lesson. Just like my major in psychology, not only do I wish to understand others, I want to understand myself.

I had encountered several people who had spent some time in a prison, but I was not given any details about their experiences while in prison. As I look back, I believe they shared their pasts only because they thought I would somehow eventually find out about their incarceration.

I truly believe they were less than truthful about the circumstances of their convictions, and I endeavored to be "polite" and not ask a lot of questions. I have come to regret not delving deeper because I now believe my "politeness" somehow belittled their experience. I now could use God's Word to enhance the purpose of their experience for a better life on earth, and potentially in eternity.

PART II
Why Prison Ministry is Needed?

The Prison House

©2016 by Brenda Simuel Jackson

The doors were about two to three inches thick,
made of steel.

The locks on the doors and the keys
seemed too big to be real.

The window of my cell was small,
covered with bars and mesh.

The air from the wind in Summer months
never made it into my home nest.

During the Winter months, ice would form
on the inside of the window pane.

It was against the rules to hang a covering over the
window to block cold air's gain.

My living space was about the length and width
of an average home's bathroom.

It was a blessing to only share one's space with one
other who did not cause one gloom.

There is no privacy, not even in toileting in your space.

Showers are communal, and you are given a specific
day and time, and you pray the shower is a time of
grace and not a time to race.

Reflections in Prison Ministry

Everything one has, not much, is counted.
You never know when a room search will occur,
don't be undaunted.

The prison house, with its rules one must follow,
is a place that makes one want to holler.

As time passes, one gains peace
in knowing that the prison house is a place
where one can learn to use time and gain release.

Prison Ministry - Needed!

"Around the globe, governments respond to illegal activity and social unrest in many ways. Here in the United States, policy makers in the 1970's made the decision to start incarcerating Americans at globally unprecedented rates. The decades that followed have revealed that the growth in the U.S. prison population can be more closely attributed to ideological policy choices than actual crime rates. The U.S. incarcerates 716 people for every 100,000 residents, more than any other country."[5]

There are approximately 2.2 million people incarcerated in American prisons and jails, and over 600,000 are released annually. The recidivism rate, those returned to incarceration has been as high as 67%. Recidivism is one of the most fundamental concepts in criminal justice. This concept refers to a person relapsing into criminal behavior after having received sanctions or undergoing intervention for a previous crime. Recidivism is measured by re-arrest, reconviction or return to prison to complete a sentence during a three to four-year period following release.

Anthony Kelley, author of *Jailhouse Religion*, found in his research that 74% of prisoners once released, were arrested within 4 years (Kelley).[6] The 1994 statistics indicated that 67.5% of the released were rearrested and 49.9% were convicted. Recent data from the

---

[5] "States of Incarceration: The Global Context." *States of Incarceration: The Global Context* | *Prison Policy Initiative*. Web. 17 Feb. 2017. <https://www.prisonpolicy.org/global/>.
[6] Kelley, Anthony. *Jailhouse Religion: The Church's Mission and Ministry to the Incarcerated*. Nashville, TN: Townsend, 1997. Print.

National Institute of Justice does not show improvement. The data reports (2014)[7] that 67.8 percent of the released were rearrested within five years of release.

Studies reported in the book, *More God Less Crime*,[8] describe re-entry programs (preparing inmates to be responsible citizens in society), as being successful in reducing the recidivism rate. These programs emphasize Spiritual growth, faith-based studies, post-secondary education, and vocational training. These studies have shown a positive impact on changing the criminal thinking process. Through Christian ministry, the need for restoration and reconciliation has become the goals of many offenders. They began to see the damages they have caused to victims of crime, family, community, and society as well as themselves. There are inmates who accept "Biblical justice, restoration through righteousness to those who received Christ."[9] I am reminded of the thief on the cross; salvation is open to all.

What is a Prison/Jail?

I have visited several prisons and jails in the State of Michigan, the countries of South Africa, Zambia, Ghana, and Swaziland. I have seen the good, the bad, and the ugly of sites called home for over 2,000,000

---

[7] Durose, Matthew R., Alexia D. Cooper, and Howard N. Snyder. *Recidivism of Prisoners Released in 30 States in 2005: Patterns from 2005 to 2010*. Washington, D.C.: U.S. Department of Justice, Office of Justice Programs, Bureau of Justice Statistics, 2014. Web. 1 June 2017. <https://www.bjs.gov/content/pub/pdf/rprts05p0510.pdf>.
[8] Johnson, Byron R. *More God, Less Crime: Why Faith Matters and How It Could Matter More*. West Conshohocken, PA: Templeton, 2011. Print.
[9] Park, Jeffrey, and W. Thomas Beckner. *Effective Jail & Prison Ministry for the 21st Century*. Charlotte, NC: Coalition of Prison Evangelists Publication, 1998. Print.

Why is Prison Ministry Needed?

souls. Several persons, whom I have spoken to about becoming involved in prison ministry, have said they don't like the idea of being locked up, hearing the doors clang shut, and not having the keys. It is the physical aspects of the prison/jail they appear to fear.

The prison house may be defined as:

   a. A place of physical bondage,

   b. A place of confinement for punishment,

   c. A place of waiting for trial or waiting for the results.

Normally prisons are not in local neighborhoods, but are in more rural areas, where transportation to and from requires one to have access to a vehicle. Many are in the middle of corn fields or undeveloped areas. The buildings are stark, with plenty of concrete, steel, wire and mesh. In some areas, the inmates never see grass or the sky. In the US, and particularly in Zambia, there is tremendous overcrowding. In one location visited, the facility was built to house 300, but at the time of our visit, 1200 were being housed. Yes, you are right; sanitation was and is a problem.

There is another prison, a prison inside the prison-house. It is a society filled with social outcast and social rejects.[10] Inmates may feel rejected, helpless, powerless, inferior, or they are among the bullies, that the leader/member of gangs. In some circumstances, there are conditions of possibly being molested physically and/or sexually. There are conditions of being morally,

---

[10] Ingram, Elijah. *The Shape of Ministry in Prison.* N.p.: n.p., 1990. Print.

emotionally, and spiritually dead. It is this prison on the inside that defines the need for prison ministry.

A report[11] by Peter Wagner and Bernadette Rabuey for the Prison Policy Initiative reports that the American Criminal Justice system holds prisoners in 1,719 state prisons, 102 federal prisons, 3,359 juvenile correctional facilities, 3,283 local jails, and 79 Indian Country jails as well as military prisons, immigration detention facilities, civil commitment centers, and prisons in US territories.

In Michigan, where most of my ministry occurs, there are thirty-three open prisons, as well as twenty facilities and thirteen prison camps which are no longer operating. Within the county there is one youth detention facility. Each county in the State has one or more jails. Where we minister there are three in the Wayne County area and one in the Macomb County area. Our team ministers monthly at four prisons, two jails, and the youth detention center. We also volunteer with Prison Fellowship and assist in special programs as requested. We have ministered at three of the closed facilities and two of the closed camps.

A common question I get from family is, "Are you going to the prison today?" The answer at any given time is, "Yes."

---

[11] Prison Policy Initiative. "Mass Incarceration: The Whole Pie 2015." *Mass Incarceration: The Whole Pie 2015 | Prison Policy Initiative.* 8 Dec. 2015. Web. 15 June 2017.
<http://www.prisonpolicy.org/reports/pie2015.html>.

Why is Prison Ministry Needed?

Who are those to whom we minister?

There is racial diversity in the prisons. Federal Statistics of those placed in supervision in 2005 provides the following pictures:

> White 41.3%
> Black/African American 31.2%
> Hispanic/Latino 21.8%
> Other 5.75%

> Gender diversity
> Male 79.7%
> Female 20.3%

Racial and other ethnic minorities are down from 64% in 2001.

Age is also a diversity variable. The ages range from 13 (youth) and up to 69+. In our local facilities in Michigan the demographics as of 2002 were:

> White 36%
> Black 40%
> Hispanic 19%
> American Indian 1%
> Asian 1%
> More than one ethnic heritage 3%
> Female 12%
> 38% 35 years or older

My personal experiences have involved a predominantly minority group (approximately 75%), with females being approximately 30%, and ages ranging from 13 to 70+, including those who have handicaps.

Campbell described the prisoner as having sociopathic tendencies[12]:

- Manipulators
- Self-centered
- Poor self-esteem
- Difficulty with value-centered goals
- Feelings of hurt
- Angry
- Fearful
- Guilty
- State of denial
- Depressed
- Lonely

I have found in ministry that it is often forgotten that the prison population include:

- Fathers
- Grandfathers
- Mothers
- Grandmothers
- Sons/Daughters
- Brothers/Sisters
- Aunts/Uncles
- Cousins/Neighbors

It is in these various forgotten roles that I am more likely to interact with the inmate. I make it a practice not to seek reasons why the person is incarcerated. I do

---

[12] Campbell, Anne. *Violent Transactions: The Limits of Personality.* Oxford: Blackwell, 1986. Print. p. 21

Why is Prison Ministry Needed?

not forget that the inmates may have some of these sociopathic characteristics. Committed crimes are often used to describe inmates. I do not attempt to validate descriptions:

- Robbery
- Sexual assault
- Homicide
- Aggravated assault
- Burglary
- Arson
- Theft
- Auto-theft
- Child pornography/molestation
- Drug trafficking
- Weapons
- Other public acts of disorder

It was found in 2002, by the Department of Justice[13] that 50% of inmates are incarcerated for violent or drug related offenses, and drug offenders are the largest source of the prison/jail population. New laws such as the "Second Chance Act,"[14] have given recognition to the unfairness in sentencing in drug violations cases. My experiences in prison ministry mirror the crimes described, but also included in the populations are

---

[13] James, Doris J. "Prison and Jail Inmates." *PsycEXTRA Dataset* (2004): n. pag. *Profile of Jail Inmates, 2002 - Bureau of Justice Statistics*. US Department of Justice. Web. 15 June 2017. <https://www.bjs.gov/content/pub/pdf/pji02.pdf>.
[14] "Bureau of Justice Assistance - Second Chance Act (SCA)." Bureau of Justice Assistance - US Department of Justice, n.d. Web. 15 June 2017. <https://www.bja.gov/ProgramDetails.aspx?Program_ID=90>.

carnal Christians, Spirit-filled Believers, other faiths, as well as unbelievers, and agnostics.

The prisons are a place for regeneration, not just rehabilitation (Kelley, p4); the prisons are a place for salvation, restoration, reconciliation, and spiritual development. I am often mindful of 2 Corinthians 2:5-11:

> "If anyone has caused grief, he has not so much grieved me as he has grieved all of you, to some extent – not to put it too severely. The punishment inflicted on him by the majority is sufficient for him. Now instead, you ought to forgive and comfort him, so that he will not be overwhelmed by excessive sorrow. I urge you, therefore, to reaffirm your love for him. If you forgive anyone, I also forgive him. And what I have forgiven - if there was anything to forgive – I have forgiven in the sight of Christ for your sake, in order that Satan might not outwit us. For we are not unaware of His schemes."

PART III
What is Prison Ministry?

Hey Chaplain

©2004 by Brenda Simuel Jackson

Hey Chaplain, didn't get that visit requested.

Hey Chaplain, can't read the print in the KJV bequested.

Hey Chaplain, who appointed you for the Lord and Master?

Hey Chaplain, will you mail this letter faster?

Hey Chaplain, when will my cup run over?

Hey Chaplain, guess what, my prayers are getting louder and bolder!

Hey Chaplain, I didn't cry last night.

I got a visit from Jesus, and not by my might!

Hey Chaplain, thanks again for helping me to see, I have a friend in Jesus,

He loves me!

Hey Chaplain!

The question is, "What is Prison Ministry?"

Ministry is to serve. Prison ministry is providing service to the incarcerated. These services meet faith-based, spiritual, emotional, mental, educational, recreational, and personal development needs of inmates. Services are provided by Chaplains and staff members in ways they deem necessary.

My major area of ministry is in-prison ministry which includes:

- Bible Study

- Worship Services including communion

- Prayer

- Spiritual development through Christian-based seminars (sample listing in appendix III)

- Writing, publishing, and distributing Christian-based books to Christian prison libraries

- Providing Bibles to Religious Services of the institutions

- Providing administrative services for Prison Fellowship International such as taking applications for Angel Tree from inmates

- Providing materials for community service projects of inmates such as yarn and beads, to make items for organizations such as Salvation Army who give them to the community

- Providing Christmas Cards to inmates to mail to their loved ones

- Helping inmates obtain birth certificates and social security cards which they will need when released

- Assisting the Chaplain in providing Speakers on issues such as addiction, victim impact, business development, and health

- Educational services include:
    - Teaching a mini-course in public speaking
    - Teaching classes on how to develop a business plan

- Provide Christian counseling as requested

- Providing physical needs such as toiletries, blankets and sanitary needs of the inmates to facilities visited in South Africa, Zambia, Swaziland, and Botswana.

What is Prison Ministry?

My 2002 Journal of Jail Ministry:

April 2, 2002:

Visitation was made to Division II, County Jail. Brenda R. was not with me, but I met members from True Faith Baptist, and we had prayer together before going to our respective areas of ministry. The Spirit was with us.

My visitation was to cell block 408 which housed eight men. Four of the inmates came to the front of the cell block for service. The other four remained in the back, but they were in ear shot of the service. Our goal was to continue our developmental courses, and we opened the session on Leadership Development, "The Leader in You." (Brenda R. and I made weekly visitations to the jail.) Our primary scriptures were 1 Timothy 1:18-20, 2:6; Acts 27:39-28:17; Exodus 18:1-27 and Matthew 5:1-5. Our objectives were to define the Christian Characteristics of Leadership and to demonstrate how those characteristics are developed and shared.

Our service started and ended with prayer. The inmates sat on the floor during the service. (No free-standing chairs were in their cells.) One inmate was concerned with the Lord granting him a release which was his prayer. We discussed this issue of faith without doubting, recognizing that all is in God's Will, and we must wait until He reveals His will to us. If God wants us to wait, remember He is with us while we wait, and He will provide all the strength necessary to get through the waiting process, and He will use us to His glory during this interim period.

All in the service (the four who came forward), professed faith in Jesus Christ.

April 13, 2002:
I met Brenda R. at Division I of the County Jail. We were continuing Moody classes and Development classes for the inmates. The officers would not admit Brenda R. to the classes; her clearance card had been pulled. This was not usual as she had just renewed her credentials. They did permit me to complete the visit.

The officer only allowed eight inmates to attend the service/class. In the past as many as 15 had been in attendance. We started with prayer. The first lesson for the Moody Class, Introduction to English, was handed out and the process of being involved in the Moody classes was discussed. Five inmates (who had not previously indicated an interest) signed up to be involved in the class. This was a special class through Moody Institute. If I or a supporter paid for one inmate to attend, nine were allowed to attend the classes at no additional cost.

We proceeded with the Developmental class/service which was on leadership, "Leaders Led By and Used By God." The scripture sources were: Genesis 12-14; Exodus 3-4,12,18; Judges 4:1-13; Acts 27:39-28:17; Esther 4:1-5:8; Nehemiah 1-5:19, and 1 Timothy 1:18-20, 2:6.

What is Prison Ministry?

We further discussed having real hope to accept the blessings of God, 1 John 5:14-15.

Thanksgiving is given to God for being used as His vehicle to equip those who may be forgotten and to share the Gospel of Jesus Christ and the Word of God. Brenda R.'s credentials will be replaced, and we are thankful. She will facilitate the class on May 4, 2002.

September 2002 visitations:
Visitations were conducted at the County jails on September 3rd, 7th, 10th, 14th, 17th, and 24th.

Restrictions have been placed on our services. We can no longer disseminate Bibles. The Bibles must be collected, and only the officers and the Chaplain can distribute the donated Bibles. I have turned in a list of names of inmates requesting Bibles, but there has not been a response. We are praying for God's intervention. The inmates believe there is a ploy to stop visitations.

Services of preaching, prayer, Bible study, and singing continued. There are always efforts to stop the Word from going forth. We comply with the rules, old and new, given by the deputies, and we believe God is making impact on the lives of some of the inmates. We were permitted to distribute booklets of the plan of salvation. Bibles were not allowed. The "Brothers", include all races, and adult ages, and some are now leading the prayer, devotion, and song. Only one has rededicated His life to Christ.

We were denied the opportunity to take the Word to another cell block, although visitation had been previously permitted.

In spite of barriers being placed, we know that God's presence has been felt during our services, and we pray His presence continues to be felt.

The attendance during our visits ranged from five to ten.

On September 24, 2002, as I was praying that God's Word be accepted and that there would be no barriers, one officer, one I describe as a "gentle soul," was cursing on the phone, loud enough for all to hear, and the other deputies were laughing. Although this is not necessarily unusual, the thought that came to me was what examples are being shown for those on the other side of the bars?

The following are excerpts of "1996 Mental Health Caregiving Model" which was part of my practicum placement with the Metropolitan Jail Ministries, for my Masters in Divinity program:

The model is specifically for the County jail system. It is only the Metropolitan Jail Ministries (MJM) which provides spiritual nurturing with the following services:

- Evangelistic Outreach
- Weekly Worship Services
- Bibles and Religious reading materials
- Bible Study

What is Prison Ministry?

- One-on-One counseling service as requested by the inmate
- Re-entry preparation classes which include group counseling/facilitation
- Individual mentoring through prayer partners and letters
- Support and assistance to families of the inmates

Due to turnover within the jails, the ministry services approximately 3000 inmates per month according to the Chaplain. The majority of those serviced by the ministry are minority males - Blacks, Hispanics, and Asians between the ages of 19 and 45. Many of the women who are incarcerated are pregnant. The educational levels range from some formal education to college graduates. The Spiritual condition of the inmates ranges from no belief in Christ and disdain of God to professed believers and ordained ministers.

Samples of typical need statements of inmates ministered to by the writer are:

- Help me stay clean
- How do I get my mother to forgive me and speak to me
- My family won't let me come home
- I have AIDS
- I was sexually abused at age 12
- My husband sexually abused my daughter
- I want to help my children

- I can't forgive my mother
- I'm scared

The proposed philosophy of counseling is based on the transient nature of the population, the environment in which the counseling is likely to occur, the lack of paid staff, a team which will be drawn from differing churches and organizations, the mission and programs of the ministry, and the clientele to be served.

The approach for providing counseling is an integration approach with Biblical truths as the foundation for assisting persons who are experiencing some type of relational crisis in their lives. This approach is based on principles outlined by Dr. Larry Crab[15] The Bible with appropriate exegesis is the guide to helping such persons. Counseling is helping the person to make choices involving their relationship with God, self, and others. The goals of counseling are adapted from Dr. Gary R. Collins, author of the book, *How to be a People Helper.*[16]

Goals:

- Help the inmate function more effectively while incarcerated

---

[15] Crabb, Larry. *Understanding People: Why We Long for Relationship.* Grand Rapids, MI: Zondervan, 1987. Print. p.59-73
[16] Collins, Gary R. *How to Be a People Helper.* Wheaton, IL: Tyndale House, 1995. Print. p. 22

What is Prison Ministry?

- Help the inmate find freedom from spiritual, psychological, interpersonal, and intergroup conflict
- Help the inmate be at peace with him/herself
- Help the inmate to enjoy a growing communion with God
- Help the inmate to develop and to maintain smooth interpersonal relationships with significant others, and with those in authority
- Help the inmate to learn and to use effective skills for living outside of the jail system, and within an environment hostile to God
- Help the inmate to be actively involved in becoming a true disciple of Christ Jesus

The statement of philosophy included:

Care-giving support incorporates the following principles based on principles from Siang-Yang Tan in *Lay Counseling*.[17]

   a. The ministry of the Holy Spirit is critical to the process
   b. The Bible is the basic guide for dealing with problems in living
   c. Prayer is an integral part of Biblical helping

---

[17] Tan, Siang-Yang. *Lay Counseling: Equipping Christians for a Helping Ministry*. Grand Rapids, MI: Zondervan, 1991. Print. p. 100-102

d. Our ultimate goal is to make disciples for Christ
   e. Our Christian Caregivers must possess personal qualities of effective caregiving
   f. The clientele's attitudes, motivations, and desires for help are crucial factors in determining change
   g. Cultural sensitivity from a Christian view is included in our approach
   h. Caregivers must be aware of their limited knowledge and skills, and know when and how to make appropriate referrals

The model included:

- Target Population
- Areas of care-giving support
- Organizational structure and staffing
- Qualifications of care-givers
- Training
- Follow-up

The practicum was completed, and the model was never implemented. The ministry was transferred from Metropolitan Jail Ministries, the chaplain accepted a position as assistant Pastor, and we continued to minister as directed by the new ministry.

What is Prison Ministry?

BSJ Christian Seminars, Inc. 501c3

In 2003, the prison ministry was formalized as a non-profit organization within the State of Michigan, and in 2007, the ministry was granted a tax exempt, 501.c3 with the IRS.

Under the umbrella of "BSJ," (short for Bible Speaks Jesus, Christian Seminars, Inc.) members from various churches or Christian organizations in Metropolitan Detroit, join together to provide prison ministry. The annual report (available online at – www.bsjchristianseminars.org) records the activities of the organization. Several of the team members have shared their call into this part of the Lord's vineyard.

The vision statement of the organization is:
- Earning Interest for God on His investment in Stewards who are imprisoned

The vision theme is:
- Transforming Uselessness into Usefulness
- To God Be the Glory.

The scriptures guiding the organization are Philemon 11-16, and Matthew 25:14-27.

The Mission is to:
- Provide an outreach ministry through the Holy Spirit's power to present the Gospel of Jesus Christ and the Plan of Salvation to those who may not hear because of imprisonment or other

types of confinement (Acts 2:24, Hebrew 13:3; Matthew 25:36)
- Provide a method of Faith-based involvement in the rehabilitation of those who are confined (Philemon 11-16)
- Provide spiritual, personal, and academic development for those who are confined (2 Timothy 3:16)
- Provide mental health care giving to help persons in crisis to improve interpersonal relationship with God, self, and others through the application and operation of Biblical constructs (2 Timothy 3:16)

PART IV
Reflections of Prison Ministry Abroad

Prison Ministry Abroad

© 2016 Brenda Simuel Jackson

The Great Commission says
go wherever there is a need for the Word.

The U.S. of A. is not the only place with prisons, jails, detention centers, and places filled with "jail birds."

All prisons around the world do not provide three meals a day or a cot on which to lay one's head.

Basic needs such as toilet paper and soap are as much of a premium as the need for a bed.

The good Samaritan has shown that loving one's neighbor is not based on having a similar background or on close geography.

Anyone in need, spiritual or physical, whether in our country or in a foreign territory abroad, is to receive ministry to their needs.

Prison Ministry is a global service
in obedience to our Lord;
ministry must go beyond our country's borders,
and provide the seeds,
and till the soil helping those who lead.

REFLECTIONS

Ministry in South Africa
January, 2011

Elder Arnoldine Lancaster, Sister Brenda M. Rudolph, and I were blessed to minister to the incarcerated in South Africa. Our visits included Durban and Pretoria, South Africa.

January 6, 2011
Our trip started at Detroit Metropolitan Airport, from which we flew to Atlanta, Georgia, from Atlanta we flew to Johannesburg, South Africa, and from there to our first destination Durban, South Africa.

The trip took approximately 16.5 hours.

January 7, 2011
Although we left the United States on the 6th, we landed in Durban the following day, the 7th. Our hosts were Prison Fellowship, Durban, the Ministry of "In His Hands," and Joshua Ministries." Our facilitators were Pastors Leon Van Assenderp and Pastor Paul Viljaen. We were housed at *Netcoral Guest House,* a bed and breakfast establishment. This was located on the beach at a reasonable cost of $67.00 USD per night, including breakfast, the shopping mall, and transportation.

January 8, 2011
We were provided transportation by Pastor Leon, and we ministered at the half-way house for male youth, who had been placed in this location by their villages, the

government or voluntarily themselves. Residents included the handicapped in wheel chairs and those afflicted with AIDS. Approximately 30 youth attended our services held under a tree, and the Lord called six (6) to confess Him as Lord and Savior. Our topic was "Self-Esteem through Jesus Christ." (A video of the service is online at the BSJ website – www.bsjchristianseminars.org. See Picture 1.)

January 9, 2011
We ministered with Pastor Leon at an inner-city church, the spiritual home of those on parole, ex-offenders, ex-prostitutes, the homeless, and those in need. The Lord spoke through each of us as we gave words of encouragement and points on overcoming. The Lord drew six (6) who confessed Christ and multiplied the donated resources, so that the collections equaled in one day what was normally collected in one month. There was enough food for all to be fed. This was a praise moment.

January 10, 2011
We visited and ministered at the Durban Female Correctional Facility (See Picture 3). We ministered in a seminar on rejection to approximately 40 female inmates. The process was interactive, and their prayers and singing truly ushered us into His presence. We were invited to return.

January 11, 2011
This was a travel day. We took a short flight to Johannesburg. Our host, Ruth Mothupi, facilitated our

accommodations in her home. Our donation for such hospitality was $50.00 (each) per night.

Ruth, known as Mimi, facilitated our purchase of ground transportation for the amount of $50.00 per day. Our host for our visitation was Pastor Douw Grobler, Executive Director of Prison Fellowship, South Africa.

January 12, 2011
We ministered at the Female Correctional Facility in Pretoria. Approximately 60 inmates attended our services, where we held a seminar regarding overcoming rejection. We were remembered by staff and inmates for our services in 2010, and we were asked to return in (2012) and to continue services.

In the evening, we visited the Provincial Hospital and ministered through prayer and the application of oil to those hospitalized and who requested same. The mother of our host was hospitalized and the father of our driver had just been released. The hospital is not up to the standards of what we know in the US as a county hospital.

January 13, 2011
The Lord's work done, we prepared to return home and traveled to the airport to catch our flight back to the US. The trip home was an 18-hour flight although the distance was shorter.

Overview

BSJ Christian Seminars, Inc. provided financial support to Prison Fellowship, South Africa ($350.00 USD), provided a donation to Angel Tree ($100.00 USD), and paid the cost of Ground transportation ($250.00 USD). All other donations, gifts, and costs were from God's three servants.

We have been invited by Prison-Fellowship South Africa to visit all 16 prisons, and specifically to visit once again Leokoup, a male and female facility visited in 2009.

We were requested to extend the visit by approximately three days to include other outreach visits, and experience some of the African culture.

We praise God, and give thanks for the prayers and assistance received in visiting Jesus in the prisons located in the utter most places of the world.

Reflections of Prison Ministry Abroad

REFLECTIONS

Prison Ministry in Lusaka, Zambia
December, 2011

Board member at Large, Evangelist Jerry Bernice Jones Davis and I, Chaplain Dr. Brenda Simuel Jackson, were blessed to be used of the Lord to minister to and to worship with the incarcerated in Lusaka and Kabwe, Zambia. Our trip began in earnest upon receipt of approval from the Republic of Zambia, Ministry of Home Affairs, to visit four Zambian prison complexes. (See picture 4 for a copy of the approved credentials.

Our journey started on Christmas morning. Jerry and I met at Detroit Metropolitan Airport. Our itinerary included a plane change in Dulles (Washington, D.C.), a fuel stop in Dakar, a plane change in Johannesburg and finally arrival in Lusaka, Zambia. We left Metro Airport at 10:00 a.m. Eastern Standard Time on Christmas, and arrived at our destination on December 26, 2011 at 9:00 p.m. (2:00 p.m. in Detroit). Our actual time in the air was about 20 hours.

We were met in Lusaka by representatives of Prison Fellowship-Zambia. Our host and guides were Pastor Paul Swala and Pastor Kwacha. These pastors spent a portion of every day as religious volunteers, meeting the needs of the incarcerated by providing food, clothing, mail, comfort, worship, prayer, and one-on-one support.

Yes, we arrived, but our luggage was still traveling. Our accommodations, including breakfast, were obtained through the Esteem Resorts Guesthouse, recommended by our hosts. Bottled water was a must for all things requiring water such as brushing your teeth.

Each of us sponsored her trip, and we are thankful for the many prayers from members of the BSJ Christian Seminars, Inc. Team.

December 27, 2011
We visited the Ministry of Health and met with Dr. Penelope Kalesha-Masumba, Child Health Specialist. She gave us assistance and directions for obtaining a yellow fever inoculation which had been recommended for Evangelist Jerry, and was necessary for a stopover in Johannesburg. Jerry was able to receive her vaccination that day "under the mango tree" in the trailer where the shots were administered. We retrieved our luggage from the Lusaka Airport and then shared a meal. We learned a few phrases in the native language: How are you? Muli Bwanji? God bless you. Mulungu akudalitseni. Good bye. Pitani Bwino.

Although our accommodations were more than adequate, the prevalence of ants and other insects required daily spraying and sleeping under a net.

Our journey continued with a morning visit to Kamwala Central Prison. I conducted worship with approximately 100 male inmates. The Lord spoke through Evangelist Jerry as she ministered to youth offenders (under the age of 21). Each service was conducted in the yard of the facility.

The afternoon itinerary took us to a Farm prison. We ministered under a mango tree, among goats, cows, and buffalo. This facility has no fences or bars, and community members use the sparse facilities. The farm houses 200 inmates. The equipment is not up to modern standards. I presented a seminar on the use of the tongue, Godly communication within the prison setting, and what is needed within society to build self-respect and esteem. Evangelist Jerry taught the use of banners and streamers as praise instruments to the Lord.

We visited the local Ministry of Health facility where a few inmates were receiving medical treatment. These inmates were ambulatory. We were not allowed out of our car, but the inmates came to the car. We ministered as God so led us.

December 29, 2011
Our journey went to Lusaka Central Prison, a facility built to house 300 but currently housed 1225 inmates. Most of the inmates were in the yard, which is about the size of a large basketball court and spectator area. It appeared that each inmate had His belongings with him, but as they sat on the dirt and on concrete ground, they sat on their belongings, and were ready for service. My sermon text was 1 Thessalonians 5:17 and Matthew 6:6-13. Jerry's lesson was from Psalm 150. Ninety-eight souls confessed Christ. Going next door, we ministered

to incarcerated women. We continued the theme of prayer and persistence. I preached from Luke 18:1-14. Jerry continued with the topic of praise. We met, you got it, under the mango trees. One inmate was nursing her child, and one was plucking feathers from a chicken, but all came for worship. There were six children "doing time" with their mothers. The Spirit of the Lord was there!

December 30, 2011
We got a very early start, 6:00 a.m., as we had a two-hour drive to Kabwe Maximum Security Prison.

On arrival, after meeting with the Officer in Charge, we ministered to the women in the medium security area. There were approximately 20 women sharing a room. Bedding was pallets on the floor. Six children were living with their mothers, and the oldest inmate was 93 years of age. Our services were held inside the women's living quarters. Prior to entering the facility, we observed visitors bringing food and other items to the prison.

After leaving the women's facility, we went to the onsite chapel. Here we ministered to 200 souls on death row. The sermon theme was divine rest, present, and future. Housed in this facility were also men serving life sentences. There was joy and peace in the chapel.

BSJ Christian Seminars, Inc. donated $1,100.00 to Prison Fellowship for the purchase of soap, sugar, salt, and toothpaste needed by the facilities visited. On return to the US, books were sent to Prison Fellowship to assist the process of spiritual growth and rehabilitation.

December 31, 2011
Today was a time to briefly visit cultural areas and local sites of Lusaka before leaving to return home. We visited the monument of the first Zambian Republican President, Dr. Kenneth David Kounda, the US Embassy, and we attended a community meeting of churches and community members who are part of the Prison Fellowship Care Group providing aid to the inmates (see picture 5). The Zambian prison system was built to house 5000 inmates. There are 53 facilities housing 16,000 inmates. Death row was built to house 40 and currently houses 240.

January 1, 2012
We shared in worship at the village church of Pastor Kwacha. The Lord once again spoke through us, provided the Word, and the Praise. The choirs of the Church truly showed their love for the Lord, and gave praise and thanks for another year.

January 2, 2012
As we prepared to return home, we were blessed to share a breakfast meal with Bishop Enocent Silwamba, Executive Director of Prison Fellowship Zambia.

We were invited by the Director to return and to minister in Ndola, Zambia where there are nine prisons.

We praise God for using us in His service.

We left Lusaka at 1:30 p.m., today (6:30 a.m. Detroit time). I arrived in Detroit at 9:45 a.m., January 3, 2012. Jerry was on a different flight.

God is good; all went well. (see appendix for a copy of thank you letter from Kansenshi State Prison).

Reflections of Prison Ministry Abroad

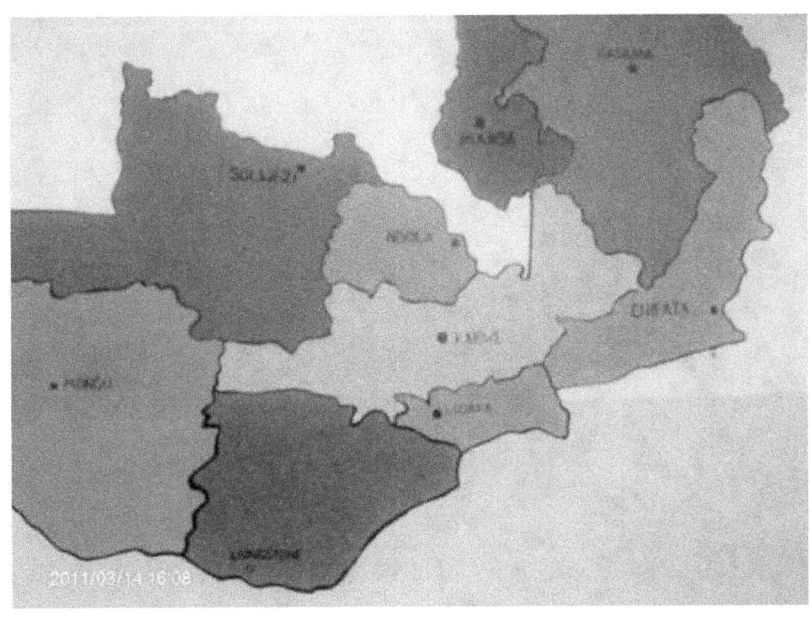

Reflections in Prison Ministry

REFLECTIONS

Prison Ministry in Ndola, Zambia
May, 2013

Ministry Team: Dr. Brenda Simuel Jackson
Sister Brenda M. Rudolph
Elder Arnoldine Lancaster

Period of Preparation

Our journey began in October, 2012 as a result of our visit to Lusaka, Zambia which ended with an invitation to minister in the prisons of Ndola, the Copperbelt region of Zambia. The invitation was from the then Executive Director Bishop Silwamba. Our credentials were submitted to the government of Zambia through Prison Fellowship Zambia (PFZ) for approval to visit and to minister within the prisons. This was a three-month process. Prayers for the journey were also initiated at this time. Our team started our as five, but only three were able to participate.

In March, after the assurance that all had been approved, there was a consecration service at Conant United Methodist Church. We purchased our tickets individually and began planning our presentations. The quilting group of Conant United Methodist Church gathered 121 throw blankets as part of our goal to meet the needs of those visited in prison. Members of Galilee Baptist Church paid the cost of shipping the blankets to PFZ to wait our arrival in Ndola. BSJ Christian

Seminars, Inc. pledged to purchase toiletry items for distribution to the inmates. Prayers were continuous.

The Trip
The route to Ndola was not direct. There was an overnight layover in Johannesburg going to and coming from Ndola. Travel time was almost 20 hours, which was 1.5 hours from Detroit to Atlanta, 15.8 hours from Atlanta to Johannesburg, and 2 hours from Johannesburg to Ndola. We left Detroit, MI on the 17th of May and arrived in Ndola on the 19th of May. There was a seven hour time difference.

We were met at the Ndola International Airport, smaller than Detroit's City Airport, by Mr. Eugene, owner/operator of the Katuba Guest House, the place of our accommodations.

May 20, 2013
Every day of our visit started with prayer and devotion. We were picked up by a PFZ representative, and we toured the offices of PFZ and met with the Executive Director, Teddy Mweetwa, and His staff. We went to a local banking establishment to exchange currency, to the local market to purchase toiletries and personal items for distribution, in addition to the blankets, face soap, towels, toothpaste, toothbrushes, washing power, glycerin, and sanitary napkins for the female prisoners, as well as books for children.

That afternoon we visited the Kensenski prison where we were blessed to minister to 200 male inmates and 28 female inmates, two with their babies. At the invitation, 30 confessed Christ. Our ministering was the Gospel and Words of Encouragement. We distributed personal items, and we also left items for over 100 men, deemed violent, to whom we did not physically minister.

This ended the first day of ministry.

May 21, 2013
Following devotions and breakfast we did additional shopping to purchase more personal items, having distributed more than planned on our first visit.

We traveled to Kamfinsa prison which houses 1,800 prisoners. We provided two services one for the male population, and a separate service for the women, six with children. As the service was open air, with no real walls to keep others from hearing, many heard the Word. In this service of all men, the National Chaplain led the attendees in the sinner's prayer and many stood for dedicating themselves to Christ. Due to the size of this population, personal items were not given.

Following a short rest and repast, we went to a Community Church and public school. The Sr. Pastor was Pastor Peter Chidoseliski, an ex-offender giving back to the community, and providing a place for other ex-offenders. The school is a one room school house, with all grades packed into a small space. There were as many as three children to a desk.

Reflections in Prison Ministry

We provided a monetary donation to the church and books for the school. At the church, Bread of Life Church, Dr. Jackson brought the Word. Sister Rudolph provided encouragement to the children at the school, and Elder Arnoldine brought prayer.

An exhausting day, but a blessed time.

May 22, 2013:
We gathered at the offices of PFZ for devotions, and we met with the Vice Chair of the Board of PFZ, Bishop Silwamba, former Executive Director.

Preparation was made for the trip to Chondwe prison, a camp, which is a place for training the inmates in agricultural skills in preparation for future release. The road to the prison was not a road, but a path overlaid with packed sand and ditches which could wreck any car. The road would only sustain one car going in one direction at a time. Hazardous driving made for a short but long trip.

Services were held outside under a tree, and the men (189) sat on the ground.

Each of us has the opportunity to speak to the group. As in other facilities, personal items were provided and blankets were donated to the prison. The officials will allow inmates in need to use the blankets, but they remain the property of the prison. The officer in charge mentioned there was a need for a prison library or reading material. It was noted that none of the inmates had a Bible. Rev. Kambungu led the congregation in a prayer of commitment. As the Apostle Paulj would say, we were richly encouraged to see the faith exhibited.

May 23, 2013
All bags are packed as we prepare for our trip home. We had a short morning service with PFZ staff, and a donation was given to the staff. We did our photo op, as pictures cannot be taken in or outside of the prisons. These pictures include the current staff: Executive Director, the Accountant who helped us shop, the young men who drove, loaded and unloaded equipment and items used in our services, Patricia who provided skills, training and coordinator who ministers to inmate families, the Secretary to the Executive Director, and Chaplain Enuch, along with our team. (see pictures #5 and #6)

Mission Anecdotes
We were invited to return to do more prison ministry. Dr. Jackson was requested to contact the Superintendant of the School of Theology, as he was interested in her teaching a seminar.

This led to an invitation to be a guest lecturer at the Theological College of Central Africa. The Superintendent, Dr. Lazarus Phiri head of Pioneers, Missiologist at Large, has offered to also assist in providing accommodations on our next visit.

On our Johannesburg layover, we visited Soweto.

Reflections of Prison Ministry Abroad

On returning home, books, and Bibles were immediately sent to PFZ for Chondwe to start its library.

We believe God was glorified, souls received salvation, needs were met and God's Will was done. We end these reflections with a song learned in Ndola.

> "I cannot do without You, I cannot do without You, I cannot do without You Lord,
>
> I cannot pray without You, I cannot pray without You, I cannot pray without You Lord.
>
> I cannot serve without You, I cannot serve without You, I cannot serve without You Lord."

Thank You Lord for using us as Your vessels, Amen.

REFLECTIONS

Prison Ministry in Ndola, Zambia
June, 2014

Chaplain Dr. Brenda Simuel Jackson
And
Rev. Dr. Ruby J. Bowens

Preparation Period
Preparation started in March, 2014 with the sending of credentials to Zambia for approval to enter the prisons in Ndola for ministry. The original team consisted of five members, but the final team consisted of two, those listed on these reflections.

Saturday, June 14, 2014
The actual mission began at Metro Airport. My day had begun with devotions, dealing with a temporary situation of no running water, and getting my dog, Sime, to the veterinarian for boarding. Dr. Bowens was attempting to visit a hospice patient before heading to the airport. BSJ Christian Seminars was blessed with a ministry donation from honorary board member, Rudolph, and then off I went to meet Rev. Bowens at the airport. Thank God for a late afternoon flight.

The Delta flight from Detroit to Atlanta was smooth, but the air temperature on the plane was, let us say, "chilly". We arrived on time, boarded our connecting flight to Johannesburg (flying time 15 hours, 26 minutes). The temperature on the plane was like 40 degrees, very cold. Blankets and a heavy sweater did not solve the cold problem. We survived the flight and arrived in "Joburg" on June 15, 2014, 5:00 p.m., Africa's time. Africa is six hours ahead of daylight savings time. We had an overnight layover in Joburg.

Through the hospitality of Minister Ruth (Mimi) Mothupi, we were hosted in the home of missionary, Shoabi Noko. We donated to their mission project in appreciation for their hospitality. We were transported from the airport by Mr. Phumulani Nyembe, and his wife. Transportation was negotiated with the help of Mimi. He also provided transportation to the airport on June 16, 2014. Our flight to Ndola was through South Africa Air. Our overnight in Joburg was a wonderful fellowship in breaking bread together, discussing missions and ministry, and having a warm bed for the night. While enjoying the hospitality of Shoabi, we checked emails, and I had a message from Prison Fellowship Zambia stating that Rev. Ruby's application to enter the prisons was still in process, and not yet approved.

June 16, 2014
Rev. Ruby and I continued our journey and arrived at the Ndola International airport. The airport is small for an international airport. There are armed guards (rifles) and baggage was handled manually. No conveyor belts. We were met by the Executive Director of Prison Fellowship Zambia (PFZ), Timothy Mweetha. We went to

the offices of Prison Fellowship, and we received a briefing on our itinerary, and met with staff.

We checked in at the Katuba Guest House where our accommodations were provided. The Guest house is owned and operated by Eugene and Winny Goss.

June 17, 2014
The accountant, Andrew, and I shopped for personal items needed by inmates and items needed by the prisons we would visit. We shopped for the needs of men, women, and children who were incarcerated with their mothers. Rev. Ruby assisted in bagging and separating items purchased. The purchases included: toothpaste and brushes for children, toothpaste and brushes for adults, body lotion to protect against cracked skin, soap for body and clothes washing, blankets, bags of salt, and boxes of sugar, sanitary napkins, and toilet paper.

In the afternoon, Rev. Enuch, National Chaplain, and I visited Ndola Remand prison, a facility similar to US county jails. Inmates are awaiting trial or sentencing. This facility housed 347 men. Approximately 200 of the inmates attended the service which was conducted in the open center area of the prison which was, surrounded by the housing units. Inmates were drying fish and laying out clothes to dry. Some inmates were standing in the doorway of their units. Most met us in the center area. Our sermon/seminar topic was "Rejection;" our Scriptures were Psalm 27:1-2, 7-10, and Romans 8:27-29, 35-37. I spoke with the aid of an interpreter who was used in all facilities except the women's.

Following my presentation, the Chaplain offered discipleship and salvation. One hundred and fifty reported making a verbal commitment to Christ.

Salt was provided to the kitchen for cooking, and the inmates received soap.

Back at the Katuba Guest House, we had for a leisurely dinner, periods of electricity going out (a regular occurrence) and rest for the next day.

June 18, 2014
After a light breakfast, we joined the staff of Prison Fellowship for devotion, songs, the word, and intercessory prayer.

The members of the staff are: Teddy Mweetha, Executive Director; Rev.Enuch Kambungu, National Chaplain; Lamson Kaunda, Driver; Margaret Seboyumba, Admin. Secy/Program Officer Micro Finance; Naomi Muskwas, Family Support Case Manager; Eraisto Chamba, Office Assistant; Patricia Chirwa, Program Officer Skills Training; Chitobu Bwakya, Family Support Case Manager; Andrew Chirwa, Accountant; Hamboya Mukundika, Program Support; and Collins Mnsona, Health & HIV & AIDS Program Officer.

Rev. Enuch and I went to the Chrondwe Prison Camp which is currently serving 191 inmates.

Reflections of Prison Ministry Abroad

Since June, 2013, BSJ Christian Seminars, Inc. has been sending Bibles, and Christian literature to the Chrondwe camp to build a religious library for the inmates. Mr. David Bibukeni, Superintendant and Officer in Charge, reports the materials are being used by the inmates and the community.

The residents of the camp come from other prisons and may be in the camp for up to two years. The emphasis is on correction, rehabilitation, and education.

It was noted that half of the men attending the service had no covering on their feet. Services were held in the open area under the one tree near the housing units. The subject of my sermon, "Repentance is More than Saying I'm Sorry," used the Scriptures 1 Corinthians 7:8-9; Matthew 5:23-24, 35. Thirty-five souls confessed Jesus Christ in response to the call. Each inmate in the facility received toothpaste and a toothbrush.

June 19, 2014:
Today we visited the town and the prison of Luanshya which housed six female prisoners and 300 male prisoners. We met the prison chaplain, and a make shift podium was set up. These services were outside in the open court area. There was an inmate praise team which led congregational singing (Africa style). The sermon of the afternoon, "Don't Turn Your Blessing into a Curse; Don't Look Back," used Scriptures from Genesis 19:15-17,23-26; Luke 17:31-33, Matthew 5:13.

One hundred and fifty of the men and all of the women attending the service confessed Christ.

The women received blankets, and napkins, and the men received lotion and toilet paper. Toothpaste and brushes were given to inmates in the hospital. A female officer requested Bibles for the officers as well as for inmates. This request was honored.

That evening we went to services at the Bread of Life Church. This is a Community Church and school plant which is operated by an ex-offender who is now a pastor. Dr. Ruby brought the evening message, "Faith, Forgiveness, and Freedom" from Colossians 3:15. Several attendees came for prayer following the message.

June 20, 2014
Our day started with a brief meeting with the Vice Chair of the Board of PFZ, Bishop Zilwamba. He prayed for us and gave his blessings.

The day's visit was to Kanseki Prison which includes males and females. The prison houses 297 men and 26 women. The PFZ Chaplain and I, were met by the Officer in Charge, and the prison Chaplain. Traveling with us was the praise team from Chaplain Enuch's ministry. They provided praises and the inmates choir also sang praises. My sermon topic was, "Saved from Condemnation of Sin," from John 3:16-21. Following the sermon, the discipleship call went forth, and 55 stood for Christ.

Reflections of Prison Ministry Abroad

The men's kitchen was blessed with 20 bags of salt for cooking. The women received blankets and napkins.

As this was Friday, the end of the work week, we went to the offices of PFZ to say goodbye to the staff.

June 21, 2014
We are going to Kanfinsa Male Program and Kanfinsa Female Program. This is the last day of our mission visit.

There are over 1900 men in Kafinsa. There is also an inmate hospital with four beds, on the ground and eleven beds off the ground. The prison praise and worship team opened the service. The chapel accommodated about 150 persons. The sermon title was, "A Taste of Triumph, from Psalm 34:6-15.

Forty men responded to the call for discipleship. The men attending the service were blessed with salt and sugar. Salt and sugar were donated to the inmate kitchen.

We left the male facility and went down the road to the female facility which houses 38 females and eight children, all under the age of five. There was congregational singing conducted by the inmates. Our Word was, "How to Touch Jesus in Troubled Times," Mark 5:21-24. Twenty-two women made their confession.

Blessings included toothpaste and toothbrushes for the children, and blankets and napkins for the women.

Prison Fellowship Zambia was blessed with a case of water and a case of toilet paper for the offices and a monetary donation for its programs.

June 22, 2014
We were on our way home. We praised God and gave Him all the glory for the work He had done. We prayed that the soil was fertile and that the seeds sown would have a hundred-fold increase. We prayed that BSJ Christian Seminars, Inc. would be able to meet needs still present.

We had a blanket, we were dressed in layers, and we were now ready for the flight home.

June 23, 2014
We arrived home safely and all is well. Praise God! Amen!

Reflections of Prison Ministry Abroad

Reflections in Prison Ministry

Reflections of Prison Ministry Abroad

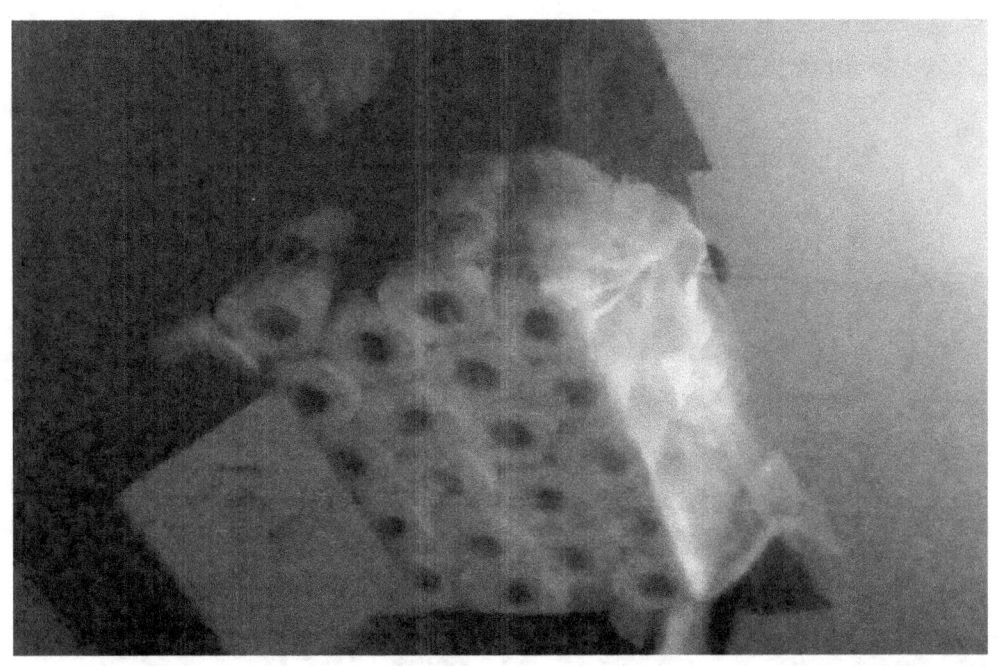

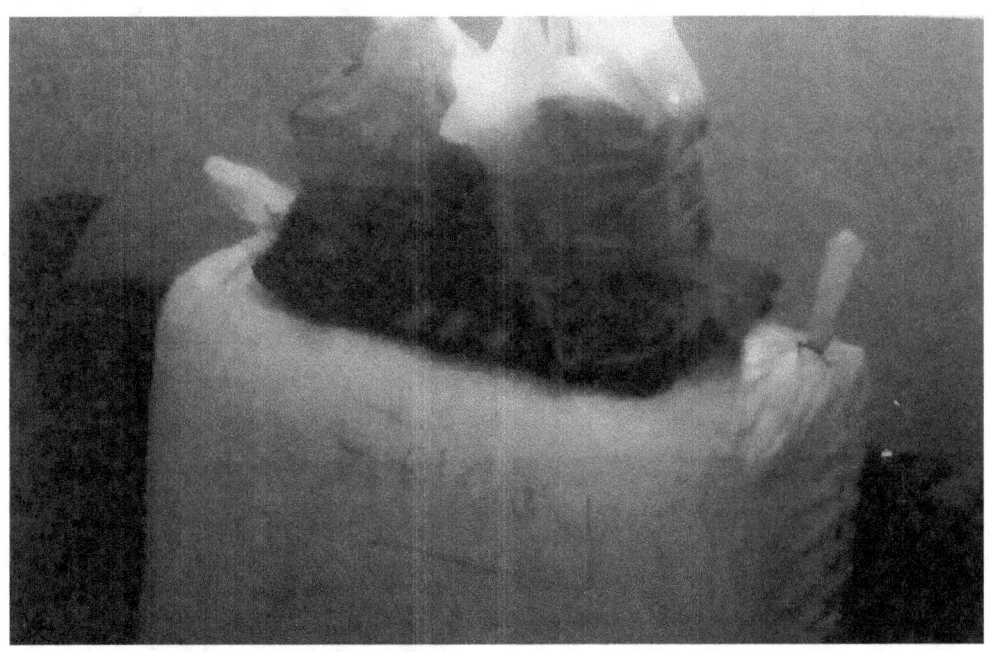

Reflections in Prison Ministry

Reflections of Prison Ministry Abroad

REFLECTIONS

The Durban Mission Journey 2015

Guiding Scriptures:

Matthew 25:36c, 40

"I was in prison and you visited me. …I assure you whatever you did for one of the least of these brothers of mine, you did for me."

Matthew 28:19, 20

"Go, therefore and make disciples of all nations, baptizing them in the name of the Father, and of the Son, and of the Holy Spirit, teaching them to observe everything I have commanded you and remember, I am with you always to the end of the age."

The disciples on this journey:

Chaplain Dr. Brenda Simuel Jackson, Rev. Dr. Ko, Sister Brenda M. Rudolph, Sister Nearline Willis, and Sister Connie Wehman.

The journey began in October, 2014 when we contacted Prison Fellowship of South Africa to assist us in getting clearances to visit the prisons, and for the World Baptist Alliance Congress for which we had registered, which was holding its 21st session in Durban, South Africa.

During the ensuing months, we planned the itinerary for our visit, and our participation in the Congress.

We started our prayer for the journey in November, and by June, 2015, fasting and prayer were the agenda.

We left our homes on July 17, 2015, as we moved toward Africa. One member of the team, Connie, was already in Africa. She is a resident of Pretoria, just outside of Johannesburg. She is the Executive Director of Prison Fellowship South Africa which includes the city of Durban, our destination.

The US team members left the US using different airlines. We met with the unexpected while in Johannesburg, when Sister Willis' luggage did not arrive, and she and Sister Rudolph missed the connecting flight from Johannesburg to Durban. This was just a couple of the many obstacles that tried to thwart the mission. God is faithful, and provided a way through every hurdle met.

By the time we landed in Durban, approximately 20 hours had elapsed since our departure from the US. You are right, it is now late evening on July 18th.

Connie met us in Durban. We rented a car, knowing that all driving including the steering wheel would be on the right side, which is opposite from cars in the US. We thank God that Rev. Daniel had experience, and in a little time he was a master at driving, and making turns without going in the wrong direction.

Reflections of Prison Ministry Abroad

During our nine-day stay, the temperature averaged 60 degrees F, needless to say, I stayed cold.

On July 20th, the team went shopping to purchase toiletries for the inmates, and food for the community church where we would minister.

On July 21st, the team drove to Pietermaritzburg, about an hour's drive from Durban. We were hosted at a medium A prison, which held medium and maximum level inmates, and housed youth ages 18 to 25, and adults. Our first stop was to provide encouragement and witness to the youth, approximately 75 inmates attended. After our witness, the young men did an African version of what we in America call "steppin." Moving on, our journey went to the adult men. We met in a room set aside for worship. Over 70 persons were in attendance including trustees, one of whom was serving three life sentences. The men provided praise and worship, Scripture and prayer, and with the aid of an interpreter, Rev. Ko and I delivered the Word. My message was "God's Forgiveness," and Rev. Ko's was "This Place is Temporary." When the invitation went forth, 35 men stood to accept Christ. Following service, each man received a bag of toiletries (toilet paper, toothbrush and paste, throw away razor, lotion, deodorant, soap, and a pair of socks.

We were surprised when the trustees and the officers provided us with an enjoyable meal.

Reflections in Prison Ministry

After leaving the prison, we visited project "Gateway" which was in the old prison and is a site used to give the needy, the poor, and the ex-offender a hand up. Job training skills, a resale shop and a temporary shelter for the homeless, are among the services provided. This is a faith-based operation.

From there we took a short trip to the train station, where Gandhi was put off of the train even though he had a first-class ticket. This was the place that Gandhi began His movement for civil rights.

We proceeded to the Community Church where, although this was Tuesday, Sunday School was conducted for the youth as an after-school program. These children live in what is called, "Squatters Village," where there is no electricity, and many houses are made of mud bricks. We interacted with the children and provided fruit (apples, oranges, bananas) and candy along with the sandwich given by the church. We also provided bags of beans and other items to the church to aid their meal program.

From the evening of the 22nd through the evening of the 25th, we attended the Baptist World Alliance Congress, where the theme was "Jesus is the Door." Over 105 countries from all over the world were represented to connect with others who believe in going forth to make disciples, love our enemies, meets needs, foster peace and reconciliation, pray, praise, and stand united in our faith.

Reflections of Prison Ministry Abroad

On July 26th, the team scattered. Connie left driving back to Pretoria, Rev. Daniel, Sisters Rudolph and Willis, returned to Pastor Peter's church for ministry to the Youth, and to visit a school, and I went to Doksa Church to preach the gospel.

On July 27th, we started our journey home, and on July 28th, we were once again in the US of A.

We give all the glory to God, Amen.

REFLECTIONS

On the Journey to Swaziland
May, 2016

Guiding Scriptures for the journey are: Isaiah 61:1; Luke 4:18,19, and James 2:15.

Isaiah:

> "The Spirit of the Sovereign Lord is on me, because the Lord has anointed me to proclaim good news to the poor. He has sent me to bind the brokenhearted, to proclaim freedom for the captives, and release from darkness to the prisoners."

Luke:

> "The Spirit of the Lord is on me because he has anointed me to preach good news to the poor. He has sent me to proclaim freedom for the prisoners and recovery for sight to the blind, to release the oppressed, to proclaim the year of the Lord's favor. [Jesus is speaking.]"

James:

> "If a brother or sister is without clothes and lacks daily food, and one of you says to him, 'Go in peace, keep warm, and eat well, but you don't give them what the body needs, what good is it? In the

same way, faith, if it doesn't have works, is dead by itself."

The Mission Team
Nkulueko (aka Leko): Member of Eagles Wings Ministries International and Kingdom Explosion Ministries, Swaziland, Africa.

Sister Faith: Member of Return to Christ Fellowship, Swaziland, Africa.

Dr. Brenda Simuel Jackson: CEO, Bible Speaks Jesus (BSJ) Christian Seminars, Inc., and Associate Minister New Prospect Missionary Baptist Church, Detroit, MI, USA.

Pastor Sizwe: Member of Prison Fellowship, Swaziland, Africa.

Sifiso Sihlongonyane: Volunteer, Prison Fellowship, Swaziland, Africa.

The Journey
Prayerful preparation for the mission began in November, 2015 by making contact with the Director of Prison Fellowship and BSJ's International Board member, Ruth Mothupi (aka Mimi), in South Africa. The Director began the process with His Majesty's Correctional Service. Mimi contacted mission members and made connections for a Church to host me at the religious services at Eagles Wings Ministries International, led by Pastor Samunenge and His wife Sibongile Mary Samunenge. All areas were

finalized in late April, 2016. The date of my scheduled departure was May 4, 2016.

Answered Prayer
On May 3rd, the day before departure, I prayed for the safety of the aircraft, the pilot, and passengers, as a prayer before departure.

I arrived at the airport a little after noon on the 4th. As I sat at the gate, the time for boarding past and the airplane was at the gate. Finally, it was announced that the flight was canceled due to mechanical problems, and the next flight would be two hours later. Too late to make my connections, I was rebooked on another flight, but due to the distance between terminals and the criteria of being at the gate at least an hour before take off for international flights, that's right, I missed that flight. I was finally rebooked for a flight the following day, May 5, 2016. I arrived in Johannesburg on May 6th. I had an overnight layover, and I arrived in Swaziland on May 7th. After the frustration wore off, I realized God had answered my prayer for safe travel.

May 6, 2016
On May 6th, I was met at the airport by Missionary Shoabi Noko. She and Mimi hosted me overnight. Both are members of Women of Africa Mission group. After a Spirit-filled evening of a meal, prayer session, and a night's rest, we hurried to the airport to board the plane for a 45-minute flight to the country of Swaziland.

Upon arrival in Swaziland, I was met by Leko and Sister Faith. We started our trip from the airport to Ezulwini, where I would be lodging at the Victory Guest House. We realized that the car rental place would not be open by the time we reached our destination. It was back to the airport for a rental car. After about 1 ¼ hours of driving, we reached the Guest House which was located behind the US Embassy. The guards refused to allow pictures to be taken. The driver for my time in Swaziland was Pastor Sizwe, who also assisted in ministering to inmates.

May 7, 2016
The team went shopping to purchase toiletries for 250 inmates housed at Piggs Peak Prison. After completion of the shopping, we returned to the Guest House, and the team bagged the items into 300 individual bags. The items consisted of toothpaste, toothbrushes, deodorant, lotion, soap, and face cloths. A community outreach was scheduled for Sunday afternoon; therefore, food stuffs, 50 bags of rice, and 50 bags of beans had been purchased, as well as candy for the children.

At the Guest House, a retreat regarding brokenness was being conducted by Tim Choo for members of Prison Fellowship International and others who worked with the imprisoned. I was able to reconnect with PFI members who had assisted me and other team members in visiting other Africa prisons: Bishop Enocent Silwamba, Regional Director of English Speaking Countries, PFI, and Walter Mashiya, previous Area Commissioner Department of

Correctional Services, Leeuwkop Prison, Prectoria, South Africa.

May 8, 2016
The day started with worship at the Eagles Wings Ministries Church. As it was Mother's Day, all mothers, including myself were honored. I gave "short words" of encouragement to the mothers, as we had to leave the service and head for "Big Bend's Community Outreach," where I was scheduled to speak. The team members accompanying me were Leko, Sister Faith, and Pastor Sizwe. As it was Mother's Day, the sermon was "Pregnant with the Gift of God," which emphasized the birthing power from within, received when we accept Jesus, The One who has no respect of persons regardless of one's station in life. My primary Scriptures were John 4:7-18, 25-26, and 39, "Jesus met the woman at the well". These services were held out of doors, yes, under a tree. There were approximately 150 adults attending and their children. The community people live in mud thatched housing without electricity, or running water. They collect wood to cook over open fire. The residents included ex-offenders and persons with positive HIV. The local pastor selected needy families to receive the food stuffs brought. To see the waving of bags of beans and/or rice was as if they were giving God a wave offering of thanks. It was a blessing to see. As we walked through the village, a mother came up to me and said, "Yes, Jesus has a plan for our future. What a Benediction!"

Leko was handing out the candy which we had purchased for the children, and she was afraid we would run out, but it was not depleted until every child received candy. God does things like that.

I thank God that my voice which was now down to a whisper, came out loud and clear during the sermon presentation. I give God the glory as He again answered my prayer.

May 9, 2016
It was a rainy day, a cold day. The team, Sizwe, Director Mandla Mtetwa, who was the Director of Swaziland's Prison Fellowship, Volunteer Sifiso, and myself, met with Assistant Commissioners of the Majesty's Correction Department of Swaziland. We were served tea and cookies, at Piggs Peak Prison. We provided three worship services. The first service was to 50 inmates who were awaiting trial. We ministered to them in their living quarters. They had floor mats and blankets for their bedding. The Sermon topic was "Repentance is More Than Saying I am Sorry", Matthew 3:2 and 18:3; 1 Corinthians 7:9, and 1 John 1:9. The Word went forth and The Holy Spirit was my microphone. When the call for discipleship went forward, 25 souls said, "Yes," to the Lord's call.

The 2nd service was held in the dining area and 100 souls attended. These inmates are serving time for convictions. The sermon topic was "Irrevocable Freedom." If the SON makes you free, you are free indeed, John 8:31-36;

Romans 8:2; and Galatians 5:1a, 16. God called 30 souls to Himself. Again, God amplified my voice.

The 3rd service was back to groups awaiting trials. There were 52 inmates in attendance. Their living quarters consisted of steel bunk beds and floor pallets. The sermon topic, "Demons are Real," was from Mark 5:12; Luke 8:26-39. If demons know the authority of Jesus, shouldn't you? Yes, God let His Word be heard, and He drew another 25 souls to Himself. We are praying that the soil was truly ripe.

Each inmate in each service received a bag of toiletries. Following the services, the Officer in Charge of the prison treated us to a repast.

Later that evening, after our team returned from the prison, the team shopped for items for the 319 inmates at Big Bend Prison. The purchases included toothbrushes, toothpaste, Vaseline, and soap; items left from the previous shopping trip were added. The team and employees of the Guest House bagged the items.

May 10, 2016
The team, Leko, Sifiso, Sizwe, and I met the Assistant Commissioner at the Big Bend Prison which houses 319 inmates. The inmates included five women, and one was carrying her baby.

The Sermon topic was, "To Truly Repent, One Must See How God Views Sin, But Still Loves Us" (Romans 5:12, 3:9-10, 23; John 8:31-36). All 319 persons attended the meeting. God is faithful, and the Word was heard, and 79 persons answered God's call.

At the end of the service, an inmate spoke words of thanks for all the inmates. He gave thanks that they were not forgotten, for the toiletries, and for the Word. He shed tears as he gave thanks. What a way to end our visit!

Mimi flew in from South Africa to join the team.

May 11, 2016
We were unable to visit the Women's facility due to special training which was being conducted. The day was spent visiting the market place, PFI office, and other sites. We were hosted for lunch by Mrs. Samunenge of Eagles' Wing Church. After lunch, we went to a prayer service at the church. The Holy Spirit was truly active, Glory to His Name.

May 12, 2016
I'm all packed, and we are headed for the airport for my flights home. Mimi and I parted in Johannesburg, and I proceeded to the USA. I just barely made my connecting flight from Dulles in Washington to Detroit, because of process and security protocol. God gave me favor.

May 13, 2016
Home again, blessings to all who prayed, contributed, and supported this ministry journey to Swaziland, Amen.

Dr. Brenda

Reflections of Prison Ministry Abroad

Reflections in Prison Ministry

Reflections of Prison Ministry Abroad

Reflections in Prison Ministry

While many are content to forget those convicted of committing crimes against society, those of us who serve God in prison ministry see precious souls for whom Christ died. Because ours is a message of hope, it doesn't matter that every prison door through which we enter must be securely locked behind us before we are allowed to proceed to the next room. As we see it, prison ministry offers an opportunity to see God's handiwork in places common folks are too afraid to enter.

For sure prison ministry is not for the faint of heart. Nevertheless, whether run by the county, state, or federal government, or even across international waters, BSJ Christian Seminars, Inc. is determined to continue offering hope, encouragement, and God's Word without compromise to those in God's mission fields behind bars.

APPENDICES

Inmate written comments

Due to privacy laws, the names of the inmates have been obstructed.

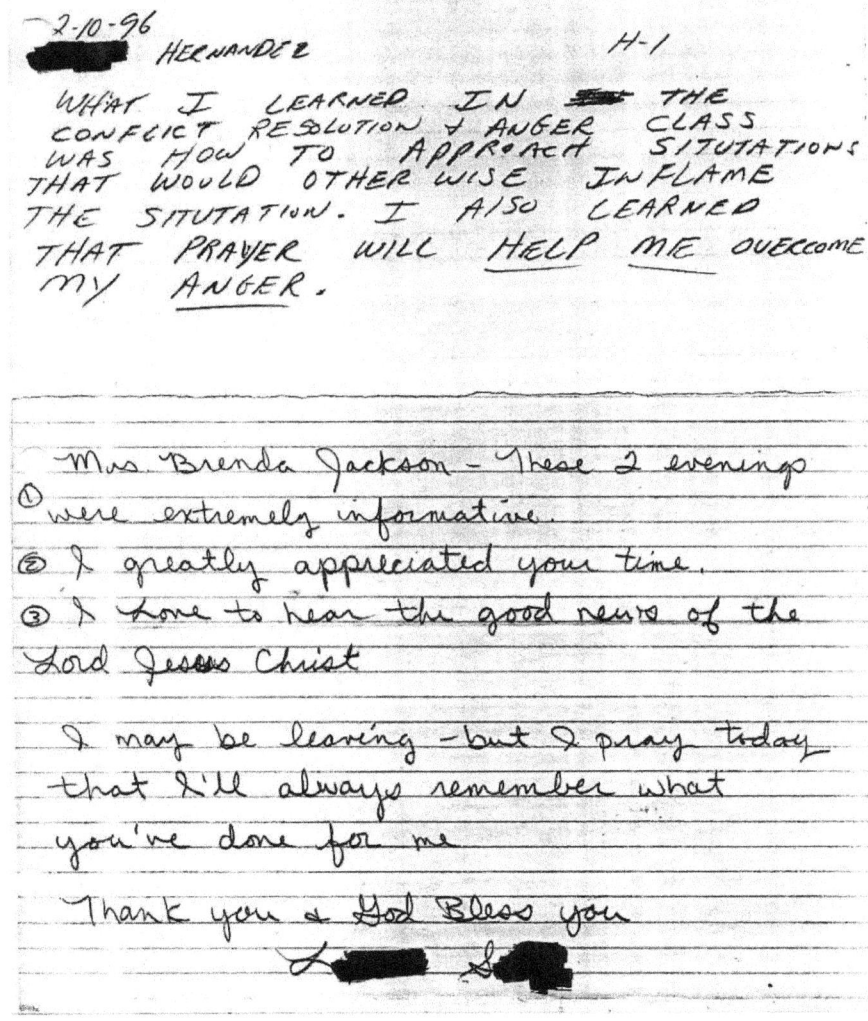

Anthony

To control my Anger.
Not to blame my Problems on others.
When me and a mate get into it, that the problem may have started with me.

How to listen and React with all senses.
That every thing things start with Jesus Christ.

That AGAPE is another word for Unconditional love.

How to solve Problems without getting Angry

To be a Peacemaker that keeps the Peace.

How to Forgive

VOTE OF THANKS: EMMANUEL NKANDU
KANSENSHI STATE PRISON

Our esteemed visitors, we as Kansenshi State-Prison we are extremely thankful for this inspiring visit you have paid us. It has brought about divine, mental, moral, revival and social motivation. As prisoners, we have felt the sense of being corrected. On behalf of the entire inmates we say may the almighty God, richly bless your ministration. Hoping to seeing you coming back to visit us again.

To our visitors, as you can see there are still some other inmates who have not dared to come and assemble with us. Therefore, we are requesting for the PIA system. If we can only have this service, will really help us to gather more inmates during our spiritual gathering. Putting the speakers outside will even enable unwilling inmates to hear the words of God amplified by the PIA system. If our request will be granted, will God reward you in abundance.

Thanks

Reflections in Prison Ministry

For more information about BSJ Christian Seminars, Inc., including Annual Reports for years 2009 through 2016, current and past seminars, along with photos from mission trips to Jamaica, Ghana, Pretoria, Ndola, Zambia, Durban and Swaziland visit www.bsjchristianseminars.org.

BIBLIOGRAPHY

"Bureau of Justice Assistance - Second Chance Act (SCA)." Bureau of Justice Assistance - US Department of Justice, n.d. Web. 15 June 2017. <https://www.bja.gov/ProgramDetails.aspx?Program_ID=90>.

Campbell, Anne. *Violent Transactions: The Limits of Personality*. Oxford: Blackwell, 1986. Print.

Collins, Gary R. *How to Be a People Helper*. Wheaton, IL: Tyndale House, 1995. Print. p. 22

Crabb, Larry. *Understanding People: Why We Long for Relationship*. Grand Rapids, MI: Zondervan, 1987. Print. p.59-73

Durose, Matthew R., Alexia D. Cooper, and Howard N. Snyder. *Recidivism of Prisoners Released in 30 States in 2005: Patterns from 2005 to 2010*. Washington, D.C.: U.S. Department of Justice, Office of Justice Programs, Bureau of Justice Statistics, 2014. Web. 15 June 2017. <https://www.bjs.gov/content/pub/pdf/rprts05p0510.pdf>.

Ingram, Elijah. *The Shape of Ministry in Prison*. N.p.: n.p., 1990. Print.

Initiative, Prison Policy. "Mass Incarceration: The Whole Pie 2015" *Mass Incarceration: The Whole Pie 2015 | Prison Policy Initiative*. N.p., 8 Dec. 2015. Web. 15 June 2017. <http://www.prisonpolicy.org/reports/pie2015.html>.

James, Doris J. "Prison and Jail Inmates." *PsycEXTRA Dataset* (2004): n. pag. *Profile of Jail Inmates, 2002 - Bureau of Justice Statistics*. US Department of Justice. Web. 15 June 2017. <https://www.bjs.gov/content/pub/pdf/pji02.pdf>.

Johnson, Byron R. *More God, Less Crime: Why Faith Matters and How It Could Matter More.* West Conshohocken, PA: Templeton, 2011. Print.

Kelley, Anthony. *Jailhouse Religion: The Church's Mission and Ministry to the Incarcerated.* Nashville, TN: Townsend, 1997. Print.

Park, Jeffrey, and W. Thomas Beckner. *Effective Jail & Prison Ministry for the 21st Century.* Charlotte, NC: Coalition of Prison Evangelists Publication, 1998. Print.

"Recidivism." *National Institute of Justice.* N.p., n.d. Web. 15 June 2017.

"States of Incarceration: The Global Context." *States of Incarceration: The Global Context | Prison Policy Initiative.* N.p., n.d. Web. 17 Feb. 2017. <https://www.prisonpolicy.org/global/>.

Tan, Siang-Yang. *Lay Counseling: Equipping Christians for a Helping Ministry.* Grand Rapids, MI: Zondervan, 1991. Print.

W. Thomas Beckner (Editor), Jeff Park. "Effective Jail and Prison Ministry for the 21st Century Paperback – 1998." *Effective Jail and Prison Ministry for the 21st Century: W. Thomas Beckner, Jeff Park: Amazon.com: Books.* COPE Publications, n.d. Web. 15 June 2017.

ABOUT THE AUTHOR

Brenda Simuel Jackson (BA, MA, Master of Divinity, Ph.D. Certified Biblical Counselor), is a born again Christian, affiliated with the Baptist Denomination. She is a member and Minister of New Prospect Missionary Baptist Church, and does ministry through BSJ Christian Seminars, Inc., Prison/Jail Ministry. She is a graduate of Wayne State University and Moody Theological Seminary – Michigan, formerly Michigan Theological Seminary. She also obtained a second doctorate in Divinity at Jacksonville Theological Seminary with a concentration in prison ministry. She is on the pastoral, pulpit, and teaching ministries of her local church.

Dr. Jackson has over thirty years of professional experience in human services, education administration, and management, as well as part-time collegiate instruction. She is currently a part-time faculty member of Wayne County Community College District. She has presented at Conferences of the American Association of Christian Counselors, local church women's retreats, mission programs, Christian

Education Institutes, State Correctional Facilities, as well as Professional and Community Programs.

Dr. Jackson is a published writer who released her first book entitled, *A Journey of Redeeming Faith,* in April 2007. It was the first of four seminar compilations entitled, *Reflections on the Path to Wholeness.* The second in the series entitled, *Being Wonderfully Made was* released April, 2008. The third in the series, *Going Through,* was released in October, 2009 and *Crossroads,* the last in this series, was released in April, 2010. In her second series, *The Ongoing Struggle* is three additional books entitled *Cross Roads* (2012)*, Freedom in a Cage* (2014)*,* and *Red Seas: Overcoming* (2016). Now she offers this work, *Reflections in Prison Ministry.* Dr. Jackson also hosted a radio broadcast, "God's Teaching Moments." Her Christian Journey includes short term outreach mission and prison ministry assignments in Japan, South Africa, Jamaica, and Ghana. Dr. Jackson also offered prison ministry in Zambia, Africa in December, 2011 as well as mid-2013 and 2014.

A native Detroiter, Dr. Jackson is a widow, a mother, grandmother, great grandmother, and ninth child of Willie and Lucy Simuel (both deceased). Dr. Jackson is a called minister of the Gospel who was licensed as a minister of the Gospel November 13, 2005. Having obtained a certification as a Chaplain; in 2013 Dr. Jackson obtained a Doctor of Philosophy in Divinity Degree with a major in prison ministry. Her vineyard is the prisons of the world.

www.ingramcontent.com/pod-product-compliance
Lightning Source LLC
Chambersburg PA
CBHW071521080526
44588CB00011B/1511